A Note to Parents & Teachers—

Welcome to I See Animals from Xist Publishing! These books are designed to inspire discovery and delight in the youngest readers. Each book features very simple sentences with visual cues to help beginners read their very first text.

You can help each child develop a lifetime love of reading right from the very start. Here are some ways to help a beginning reader get going:

 Read the book aloud as a first introduction

 Run your fingers below the words as you read each line

 Give the child the chance to finish the sentences or read repeating words while you read the rest.

 Encourage the child to read aloud every day!

Published in the United States by
Xist Publishing
www.xistpublishing.com
24200 Southwest Freeway
Suite 402-290
Rosenberg, TX 77471

eISBN: 978-1-5324-1416-9
Saddle Stitch ISBN: 978-1-5324-1487-9
Perfect Bound ISBN: 978-1-5324-4209-4
Hardcover ISBN: 978-1-5324-3406-8

© 2020 by Xist Publishing
All rights reserved
No portion of this book may be reproduced without express permission of the publisher
All images licensed from Adobe Stock
First Edition

I See Animals
Fish

written by August Hoeft

I see a fish.

The fish is yellow.

The fish is very colorful.

The fish eats fish food.

The fish lives in the water.

Things to do next!

Write a Sentence

I see a _____.

Drawing

Make a drawing of your favorite animal.

Sharing

Talk to your classmates about your favorite picture in this book. Explain to them why you like it.

WORD LIST

a	is
colorful	lives
eats	see
fish	the
food	very
I	water
in	yellow

Have you read the other I See Animals Books?

- Alligator
- Bear
- Beaver
- Butterfly
- Cat
- Cheetah
- Chicken
- Chinchilla
- Chipmunk
- Cow
- Deer
- Dog
- Dolphin
- Donkey
- Duck
- Eagle
- Elephant
- Elk
- Ferret
- Fish
- Fox
- Frog
- Giant Panda
- Giant Tortoise
- Giraffe
- Goat
- Gorilla
- Guinea Pig
- Hamster
- Hedgehog
- Hippo
- Horse
- Jellyfish
- Kangaroo
- Kitten
- Lemur
- Lion
- Lizard
- Llama
- Love Bird
- Meerkat
- Monkey
- Moose
- Mountain Lion
- Mouse
- Octopus
- Orca
- Owl
- Panda
- Parrot
- Penguin
- Pig
- Polar Bear
- Puppy
- Rabbit
- Raccoon
- Rhino
- Sea Lion
- Sea Turtle
- Shark
- Sheep
- Snail
- Snake
- Squirrel
- Squirrel Monkey
- Tiger
- Tree Frog
- Turkey
- Turtle
- Whale
- Wolf
- Zebra

www.ingramcontent.com/pod-product-compliance
Lightning Source LLC
LaVergne TN
LVHW070015090426
835508LV00048B/3414